Say More with Less

Say More with Less

Adeola Awe

Adeola Awe
heavensentient@gmail.com
Find me on Instagram:
@heavensentient
@saymorewithless
www.saymorewithless.org

ISBN: 979-8-9877599-0-5 (paperback)

ISBN: 979-8-9877599-1-2 (eBook)

Printed in the United States of America

First Printing: February 2023

Contents

This project is dedicated to
those who have preceded me
and to those who will succeed me
and succeed indeed.

Less dense
I give utmost reverence
to Opulence.
The Essence
that lessens
the tension
and faultiness
of five-sense perception
of this experience.

5

A foundation cannot sustain
on uneven terrain.

How do you deprogram
when you're deep in the program?

Confront that which stunts.

Peel back the rind
to the core.
The sore truth ignored not.
No matter how por-ous
you may feel,
the veil no longer conceals
the hurt.
Birthed through pain,
the pleasure
immeasurable.
No longer tethered to whether
you should shoulder the burden
or remove the boulder altogether.
Start anew with an ace
not a trace of the distaste
stomached.

I'm playing a game
with no clear objective,
impartial to whether I win
or simply meet the bare min.
My limbs fatigued
from futile attempts to advance
against the current,
a deterrent,
pushing me toward a fut-ure
I can no longer re-fute
and away from a past
never intended to last.
Self-imposed torture
I refuse to endure
lest I mourn the loss
- opportunity cost -
of what could be
for the familiarity
of the present,
a transient gift
I've come to resent.

There's a part of me
unwilling to part
with a cultural script
that ought to be ripped to shreds
and laid to bed
lest I spend my waking hours
in dread,
blindly led and underfed.
Malnourished,
unable to flourish
into my final form.
Torn between an ideal
and a real-ity
born into and conformed.

I'm nearing the end of a time
where I cease to revere nor identify
with wants not inherently mine,
confined to another's storyline
unless I choose an alternate route
better-suited
for my passionate pursuit
toward ripe fruit
with no gripes nor rues
about what I should and should not do.
My Tower isn't structurally sound.
I'm found bare,
hyperaware,
scared of the turbulent ground.
"There's no need to be frightened,"
says the dark night.
"You have the keys to enlighten
and become One with The Light."

3

Don't condemn nor condone.
To each their own.

How does one interact
but not distract oneself from
the known fact
that most act
in order to catch contact?

Any opponent with intent to harm
will be disarmed.

You'll wreck
if you break your neck
to check
how far others have trekked.

7

Give no reactions to distractions.

Take time
to comb through
and prune.
Soon,
you'll fine-tune
your worldview
no longer misconstrued
by the news-ance.

I've gradually become
numb
to the humdrum
web of lies spun.
There's no air to vent
nor lament
about events designed
to prevent the Ascent.

4

Become less reliant
on the advice
others have acquired.
Confusion comes
when you admire
a choir.
Believe in your Power
that doesn't cower
behind material desire
laced in copper wire.
Trust that Source
will keep you on Course.
Withdraw from discourse
that is surface.
You'd be doing yourself
a disservice.

The layperson
versed in
Knowledge easy to recite.
Not quite
ready to bite
The Apple
of delight and fright
despite what might
occur.
The obscurity
of the unknown may lead to
Light or night.
Which is Right?

No one should speak
on areas that they,
themselves, are weak.
The ensuing hypocrisy
lends itself to deceit,
crafting an illusory image
as one holier than thee.

You know
yet act slow.
Truth in tow
but for show,
No?
Sow reaps no grow.
Cuidado
before you throw
what's been bestowed.

Don't allow yourself to be led
by a less credible source.
Oh, the remorse
when you realize you've been
force-fed lead
and divorced
from the best possible Course.
Keep steadfast ahead
and tread seamlessly with The Force.

Many utter words premature
I'd like to ensure
that what I posit is
matter-of-fact
integrity intact
not lackadaisically supposed
haphazardly composed
prose.
Better to be mute
than stutter half-truths
that can be easily disputed
Absolutes cannot be refuted.

Don't heed the advice
of someone on speed.
Free yourself from the need
to seek reprieve externally.
The Eternal is the ultimate Voice,
capable of directing you
toward choices
that propel you forward
with minimal noise.

6

Being dependent on
someone or substance
has you feeling
lonesome and depressed,
which causes
unnecessary stress.
You can change that narrative.
It is imperative
that you don't regress.

The past
comes to disturb
my present
its presence
- unwelcome -
feelings resurface
as if induced by
a recent cause.
My peace
now pieced apart
by hurt unresolved.

As pleasures surge
curb the urge
to visit old tombs,
open scarred wounds
without consulting Reason.
Many come for a season
as a test.
One is encouraged
to progress
with less(ons).

I don't subscribe to bribery
enticed by vices
surefire way to demise.
Suffer today
for a thriving tomorrow.
What a sorrow-filled life.
Don't consent to strife
before you find yourself
resentful,
stifled by the flame
of an inhumane,
sadistic game.

Malevolent forces
cause my flesh such torment.
Feelings once dormant
erupt,
disrupting my calm.
My Spirit, a soothing balm.
My writing, a healing psalm
to quiet my writhing qualms.

People don't exist
until your gaze becomes fixated
on another.
Allow the memory to dissipate
with not an utter.
The bliss will be dearly missed
and subsequently dismissed
with no reminisce.
Smothered.
Go ghost,
become engrossed in
your own story
unlike most
who scroll mindlessly through posts
into an abysmal hole
with no end goal.
Devoid of feeling whole.

11

Refrain from displacing blame
when you *knowingly*
stepped foot into the flame.
You had the foresight to avert pain.
Tame the lion's mane
before you defame your name.
Allow the temptation to wane
before the shame remains.

Through disciplinary action
one develops discipline
and strengthened intuition,
prompting one to listen
to the voice with-in
for any premonition.
Don't let causes affect (v.)
your affect (n.),
resulting in effects
that are difficult to neglect.
Eliminate the cause
and soon you'll find resolve.

Don't overcomplicate
the simplified.
In time
you'll learn
to discern
and refine
as you align
with The Divine
and mine
to the depths of the crystalline.

Don't move with haste
before you waste an opportunity
if not properly paced.
There's no race to be won.
Tread gracefully, knowing
there's nothing to be done.

It feels like déjà vu.
Thankfully,
I assume an aerial view,
so I can examine
my subjective objectively
with a perspective unskewed.

Picture this:
pressing matters take precedence
and matters irrelevant
recede into the recesses
of my mind
purely afterthoughts,
residing in the hind
not at the forefront
of conscious perception,
trying to beckon
for my attention.
Either you grab ahold
of the reins and steer
or fold and veer
down a path unclear,
driven by impulses that reign supreme
while you remain passive
like passersby inactive.

Sever ties
with past lives/lies
before you meet
your inevitable demise.
No longer mesmerized
by impermanent highs.
Reside
in the all-knowing Eye,
Realized.

About the Author

Adeola Awe is an Afro-Caribbean American, who presently resides in the state of Georgia. She has obtained both her B.S. in Neuropsychology as well as her 200-hour registered yoga teacher training (RYTT) certification. She considers herself a realized Libra Sun and, most importantly, a newfound creative with the aim of healing others through varied mediums.

Find Adeola at her website **www.saymorewithless.org** and on Instagram **@heavensentient** and **@saymorewithless**.